Debbie Weiss

The Sprinkle Effect

workbook

Engaging Exercises and Thoughtful Prompts to Support Your Journey to a More Colorful and Fulfilling Life

The Sprinkle Effect Workbook

Cover Design: Shana Recker
Interior Design: Jason Recker Design

Paperback ISBN: 979-8-9910847-0-3

Congratulations!

You've just taken the first step to living a more colorful and fulfilling life. The fact that you're reading this tells me that you are in search of something—some answer.

Over a decade ago, I found myself wondering, *is there any more to life?* It wasn't necessarily that my life was awful. Of course, I had my share of challenges that seemed to just keep coming, but doesn't everyone?

I realized **if my life ended at that moment, I would have had regrets**. Regrets that I hadn't lived my life to the fullest, but I had no idea what that meant.

It wasn't like I had any passion or goal that was lying dormant inside me, longing to be exposed. I wished I did, but it was more like a nagging feeling; that we only get one shot at this game of life, and I wanted more for myself.

The trouble was I didn't know how to figure out what the "more" was... and even if I did discover it, **what could I do about it?**

There seemed to be other people who were happy and fulfilled and I yearned to know how that felt. *What made those people so special or different from me?* If they knew the secret, then I knew I could figure it out as well.

So, my quest began!

It's been over a decade since I embarked on my search and I'm thrilled to report that **I found the answer that quenched my thirst**. It's not an answer I can reveal in a single sentence, because it's different for each of us. I learned **it's all about the journey**: the journey of truly discovering yourself. ***But it takes work.***

You can't just read a few books and *voila!* you're a new person. I'm guessing that's why many of us never uncover the key. But luckily, that's not you.

You **are ready to do the work and I'm here to provide you with the framework.** I'd like to officially welcome you to your personal journey of adding "sprinkles" to your life!

Just as sprinkles transform an ordinary dessert into something extraordinary with color, texture, and excitement, this workbook will guide you through adding metaphorical sprinkles to your daily life. We'll explore how **small, positive changes can brighten your mood, boost your satisfaction, and turn the ordinary into something special**.

In the following pages, you'll discover how to:

- Shift your mindset,
- Let go of limiting beliefs,
- Take purposeful action, and
- *much more!*

Each exercise in this workbook represents a new "sprinkle"—a small but but impactful change that can **make your life more vibrant and fulfilling**. They are character traits you can develop and step into on your journey. As you progress, you'll find yourself **waking up with growing excitement, eager to add another sprinkle to your day**.

Are you ready to create a more colorful, satisfying life?

Grab your spoon *(a pen!)* and **get ready to create new possibilities in your life—one colorful sprinkle at a time**.

Table of Contents

How to Use this Book   5

1. A Sprinkle of Perspective   6

2. A Sprinkle of Mindset   16

3. A Sprinkle of Belief   23

4. A Sprinkle of Courage   31

5. A Sprinkle of Responsibility   39

6. A Sprinkle of Dreams   49

7. A Sprinkle of Direction   58

8   A Sprinkle of Vision   66

9. A Sprinkle of Action   75

10. A Sprinkle of Discipline   84

11. A Sprinkle of Adaptability   93

12. A Sprinkle of Resilience   102

13. A Sprinkle of Curiosity   112

14. A Sprinkle of Connection   120

15. A Sprinkle of Joy   130

A Letter from the Author   138

About the Author   155

How to Use this Book

This workbook is the companion to my book, *The Sprinkle Effect: A Guide to Creating a More Colorful and Fulfilling Life*. However, it can also be used as a standalone workbook. If you are using it without reading the book, I will provide a brief overview of each chapter for you.

The Sprinkle Effect provides a more detailed explanation along with personal stories to illustrate each sprinkle. The activities and journal prompts are taken directly from the book. In addition, you will find some new journal prompts that are not in the book. Feel free to pick and choose which prompts resonate with you.

The idea of using a journal prompt is to get you thinking about a particular topic. It gets the wheels turning on subjects you otherwise may not have reflected on before. If you're anything like I was, you might be thinking, *why do I need to actually write? Instead, can't I just think about my answer?* You certainly could, but putting pen to paper really helps bring clarity. I find that when I write, I surprise myself with my answers. I learn that I am actually thinking about certain things or in a certain way that I was completely unaware of. You'll also find that it's useful to go back and revisit these prompts. Just because you answered one way a few months ago, doesn't mean you'll have the same answer today.

If you can't tell, I'm an enthusiastic fan of journaling. So even if you're not, humor me and give it a try.

Just as there are a variety of sprinkles, there are a variety of ways you can use this workbook in conjunction with the book:

1. Read the book from cover to cover without stopping to do the exercises. You can then go back and slowly tackle the exercises you feel would be beneficial.

2. Read a chapter, then open this workbook to the corresponding chapter and complete the exercises before moving on to the next. You most likely want to leave some time before moving forward so you have enough time to digest that particular sprinkle.

3. Only read the chapters you feel you need, then complete the exercises in this workbook. Maybe you already have orange, teal, and blue in your jar of sprinkles. If so, skip to those colors you desire the most.

4. Once you're done and you have the whole rainbow in your jar, refer back to your prompts and answers when it feels like one of the colors is dimming. I've left extra pages at the end of each chapter and at the back of the workbook to use as you wish. This is the perfect place to revisit activities and journal prompts.

In the past, I've purchased countless books and workbooks that I partially completed, threw in a pile, and years later, donated. Can you relate? **It's time to change that pattern.**

If I told you I held the magic potion to create a fulfilled life, ***would you drink it?*** I sure would.

This is your magic potion, the difference is it's not something you can drink. You need to put in the ***work***, but I promise **it will be worth it in the end.**

Remember, this is your one and only life! It's up to you how it plays out.

1

A Sprinkle of Perspective

> **Blue:** Often associated with depth and stability, blue can represent a broad and deep perspective.

Perspective is the lens through which we view all our experiences. It's often difficult to step back and realize that our perspective is not necessarily correct or that someone else's perspective is not necessarily wrong. Our perspective comes from the sum of our beliefs, values, and experiences. When we truly open ourselves up and listen and consider others' viewpoints, we can begin to change our lives. When we put on a new pair of glasses, with different lenses, a whole set of new possibilities we never considered before becomes available to us.

Key Takeaways from *The Sprinkle Effect*

1. **Perspective Shapes Our Reality:** Changing how we view our roles and responsibilities can profoundly impact our happiness and effectiveness.

2. **Embracing Different Viewpoints:** Recognizing that others may have valid perspectives can broaden our understanding and enrich our interactions.

3. **Openness to New Perspectives is Key:** Being willing to reconsider our viewpoints can lead to significant personal growth and improved relationships.

Activities

Activity 1: Reframing Exercise: Shifting Perspective

Objective

Practice the skill of reframing by changing negative or unhelpful thoughts into more positive, empowering ones.

Step 1: Identify the Negative Thought

- Write down a specific negative thought you've had recently. It could be about yourself, your abilities, a situation at work, or a personal relationship.

  Example: "I never do anything right."

_____

_____

_____

_____

Step 2: Challenge the Thought

- Ask yourself a series of questions to challenge this thought. Is it really true? What evidence do I have to support this thought? Is there evidence that contradicts this thought?

  Example: Have there really been no instances where I've done something right? Can I think of a time when I succeeded at something or received positive feedback?

_____

_____

_____

_____

_____

_____

_____

_____

_____

_____

_____

_____

_____

Step 3: Identify the Trigger

- Reflect on what triggered this negative thought. Understanding the context can help you see patterns and situations that often lead to negative thinking.

   Example Trigger: Maybe the thought arises when you're trying a new task at work or after a conversation with a particular person.

_____

_____

_____

_____

_____

_____

Step 4: Reframe the Thought

- Transform the negative thought into a more positive or neutral one. The reframed thought should be believable and based in reality. It's not about creating a false sense of positivity but rather finding a more balanced view.

   Reframed Thought Example: "While I sometimes make mistakes, I also have successes. Everyone has areas to improve, and I'm working on mine. I learn from my mistakes and celebrate my achievements."

_____

_____

_____

Step 5: Reflect on the Reframe

- Consider how the reframed thought makes you feel compared to the original negative thought. Does it reduce stress? Does it feel more empowering? Reflection can help reinforce the value of reframing.

_____

_____

_____

_____

_____

_____

_____

Activity 2: Media Diversity Audit

Objective

Broaden your understanding and perspective by exposing yourself to different viewpoints and cultural narratives through diverse media sources.

For one week, consume media only from sources outside your usual choices (e.g., if you usually watch mainstream news, try independent outlets; if you read Western authors, choose authors from other parts of the world). Note any differences in viewpoint and information presented.

_____

_____

_____

_____

_____

_____

_____

_____

Activity 3: Empathy Exercise

Objective

Practice seeing situations from another person's perspective to enhance empathy and understanding.

Step 1: Identify a Situation

- Think of a recent conflict or misunderstanding you had with someone. It could be a minor disagreement or a more significant issue.

_____

_____

_____

_____

Step 2: Write Your Perspective

- Write down your perspective of the situation. Describe what happened, how you felt, and why you felt that way.

_____

_____

_____

_____

_____

_____

_____

Step 3: Shift to Their Shoes

- Now, write down the same situation from the other person's perspective. Imagine their feelings, thoughts, and motivations. Why might they have acted or reacted the way they did?

_____

_____

_____

_____

Step 4: Find Common Ground

- Identify any common ground or shared feelings between your perspective and theirs. What can you learn from seeing things from their point of view?

Step 5: Reflect on the Experience

- Write a reflection on what you learned from this exercise. Did it change your understanding of the situation? How can this new perspective help in future interactions?

Journal Prompts

- Identify a major life change you've experienced. Write a few sentences on how your perspective shifted before and after this change. What new insights did you gain?

- How do you typically react when someone disagrees with you? Write about a time when you considered their perspective and what you learned from it.

- Choose a belief or opinion you hold strongly. Why do you believe this, and what experiences have shaped this perspective?

- Describe a time when you felt misunderstood. How might the other person's perspective have influenced their misunderstanding of you?

- How do your cultural background, upbringing, and experiences influence the way you see the world? Identify a specific example where your background shaped your perspective.

- Consider a problem you're currently facing. List at least three different perspectives from which you could view this problem and note what each perspective might suggest as a solution.

"I've realized that seeing things from a different perspective isn't just about changing your view, it's about opening doors to growth and new possibilities."

DEBBIE WEISS

2

A Sprinkle of Mindset

Silver: Shiny and reflective, silver sprinkles can symbolize the clarity and brightness of a positive mindset.

A growth mindset is essential for personal development and success. It involves viewing challenges as opportunities for learning and believing that abilities can be developed through dedication and hard work. Cultivating a growth mindset encourages continuous improvement, resilience in the face of setbacks, and the pursuit of long-term goals. This positive outlook transforms failures into steppingstones and promotes a lifelong love of learning.

Key Takeaways from *The Sprinkle Effect*

1. **Transformative Power of Mindset:** Shifting from a fixed to a growth mindset expands possibilities and impacts outcomes.

2. **Challenges as Growth Opportunities:** Embrace challenges as chances to learn and grow, not just obstacles.

3. **Importance of Self-Awareness:** Use tools like journaling and mindfulness to increase self-awareness and guide your mindset transformation.

Activities

Activity 1: Create Your Own "Maybe I Can" List

Objective

Reflect on your past achievements and survivals to build confidence and resilience. Keep this list accessible for moments when you need a reminder of your capabilities and growth.

Make a list of all the things in your life that you survived and/or accomplished. I recommend keeping the list somewhere easily accessible, such as on your phone or computer, so you can refer back to it often.

Activity 2: The Power of Yet

Objective

Shift your mindset from fixed to growth by adding "yet" to self-limiting statements. Track these instances and reflect weekly to recognize how this small change impacts your perception of challenges.

Whenever you catch yourself saying "I can't do this," add "yet" to the end. Write down these instances and reflect on them at the end of the week. How does adding "yet" change your feelings about the challenges?

_____

_____

_____

_____

_____

_____

_____

_____

Activity 3: Skill Development Commitment

Objective

Break through the fear of failure by committing to a new skill or habit, dedicating manageable time segments consistently over three weeks.

Pick a new skill you've wanted to learn but have avoided due to fear of failure. Dedicate a small, manageable amount of time three days a week to learning this skill. Commit to trying this for three weeks. Document your progress and setbacks, focusing on what you learn from each.

Week 1

_____

_____

_____

_____

_____

_____

Week 2

_____

_____

_____

_____

_____

_____

Week 3

_____

_____

_____

_____

_____

_____

Journal Prompts

- Describe a time when you encountered a challenge and felt defeated. How might approaching this challenge with a growth mindset change your perspective and actions?

- Think about an area of your life where you feel stuck. What steps can you take to shift from a fixed mindset to a growth mindset in this area?

- Take a moment to list five things you've learned from past failures. How have these experiences contributed to your growth?

- Think about a recent conversation where you expressed self-doubt. How can increasing self-awareness help you change the way you talk about yourself and your abilities?

- Describe how you react to constructive criticism. How does your current mindset influence these reactions, and how can you use these criticisms to foster growth?

- Write about a time when you helped someone else through a challenging situation. How did this experience impact your own mindset and perspective on challenges?

"Your mindset is the driving force behind everything you do. It determines how you perceive situations, how you approach challenges, and ultimately, how you succeed or fail."

TONY ROBBINS

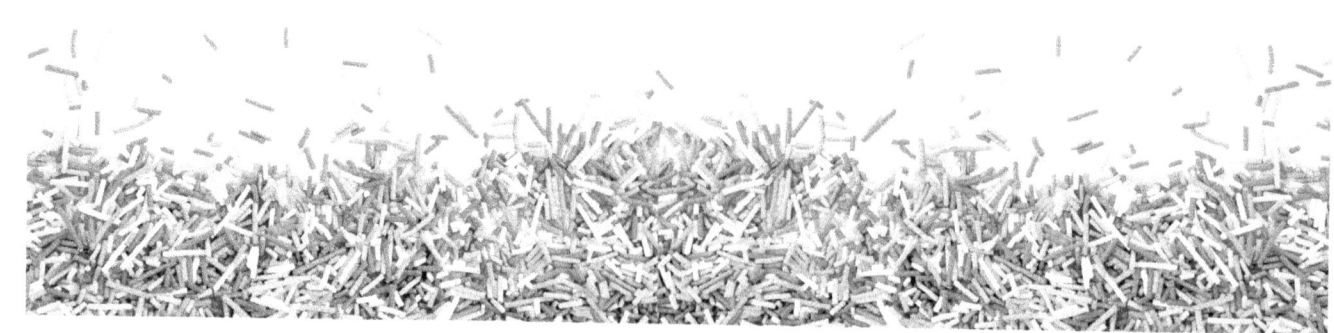

3

A Sprinkle of Belief

Gold: Precious and valuable, gold represents the foundational beliefs that support and enrich our lives.

Beliefs shape your reality, influencing how you see the world and your place in it. Identifying and challenging limiting beliefs can transform them into empowering thoughts that support your goals. Reframing your beliefs fosters self-confidence, encourages risk-taking, and paves the way for greater personal achievement and fulfillment. This process allows you to break free from self-imposed limitations and realize your full potential.

Key Takeaways from *The Sprinkle Effect*

1. **Spotting Limiting Beliefs:** The reasons we often doubt ourselves, like feeling scared or not good enough, develop early and stem from what we learn from parents, teachers, and friends.

2. **Changing Our Brain:** Our brain can learn new ways of thinking, which means we can change old doubts into positive thoughts that help us do better.

3. **Being Honest with Ourselves:** It is important to pay attention to our own thoughts and actively change the negative ones so we can truly achieve what we're capable of.

Activities

Activity 1: Belief Flip Exercise

Objective

Identify and challenge limiting beliefs by reframing them into empowering ones.

Step 1: Identify the Limiting Belief

- Write down a specific limiting belief you have about yourself.
  Example: "I'm not good enough to achieve my goals."

_____

_____

_____

Step 2: Evidence Examination

- List evidence that supports this belief.
  Example: "I failed a project at work."

_____

_____

_____

Step 3: Contradictory Evidence

- List evidence that contradicts this belief.
  Example: "I successfully completed several projects in the past."

_____

_____

_____

Step 4: Reframe the Belief

- Transform the limiting belief into a more empowering one.
  Example: "I am capable of achieving my goals with the right effort and mindset."

_____

_____

_____

Step 5: Affirmation Creation

- Create a positive affirmation based on the new belief.
  Example: "I am capable and can achieve my goals."

_____

_____

_____

Reflection

- Reflect on how this new belief makes you feel compared to the old one. Write down any changes in your mindset or emotions.

_____

_____

_____

_____

_____

_____

Activity 2: Positive Affirmation Replacement

Objective

Replace negative self-talk with positive affirmations, fostering a more optimistic mindset.

Stop speaking to yourself so negatively. Every time you catch yourself saying something negative, tell yourself three positive things instead.

Activity 3: The Five Whys

Objective

Identify and understand the root cause of a limiting belief in order to effectively address and overcome it.

Take one of your limiting beliefs and ask yourself *"Why do I believe this?"* Write down the answer, then ask *"Why?"* in response to that answer.

Repeat this process five times to get to the root cause of your belief. Understanding the deeper reason behind a limiting belief can help you address it more effectively.

Journal Prompts

- Think about a limiting belief you've held about yourself. Write a "before and after" story showing how this belief has limited you and how changing it will (or has) set you free.

- Think of a time when you succeeded despite doubting yourself. What did you learn from that experience about your own capabilities?

- Write about a belief you acquired from your family or peers that you now realize is holding you back. How can you begin to change this belief?

- Reflect on a moment when you felt you weren't good enough. What would you say to your younger self in that situation, knowing what you know now?

- Describe a recent situation where you felt the burdens of success were too heavy. How can shifting your belief about success and its burdens change your approach to achieving your goals?

- Consider a belief you've held since childhood. How has this belief shaped your actions and decisions over the years? What new belief would you like to replace it with, and why?

"These beliefs are simply thoughts you've been thinking about over and over again, so you believe them to be true. One of the great things about our brain is that it is neuroplastic, so we have the ability to reprogram it regardless of our age."

DEBBIE WEISS

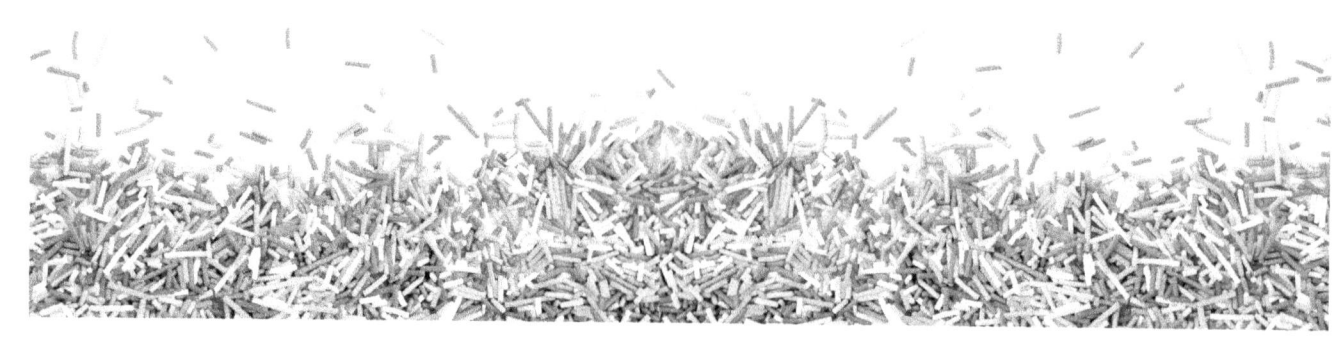

4

A Sprinkle of Courage

Red: A bold and powerful color, red embodies the strength and bravery inherent in courage.

Courage isn't about the absence of fear, but about taking action despite it. Building courage involves taking small, brave steps that gradually increase your confidence and help you tackle larger challenges. This process leads to significant personal growth, as each act of courage reinforces your belief in your ability to overcome obstacles. Embracing courage helps you live a more adventurous and fulfilling life.

Key Takeaways from *The Sprinkle Effect*

1. **Fear Is Natural, Courage Is a Choice:** Embrace fear as a part of life, but recognize that stepping beyond it to pursue new opportunities is where true growth and transformation happen.

2. **Small Acts of Courage Build Confidence:** Regularly facing fears, even in small ways, strengthens your confidence and proves to yourself that you can handle challenges.

3. **Growth Through Discomfort:** Stepping out of your comfort zone is essential for personal development and achieving your full potential.

Activities

Activity 1: The Courage Challenge

Objective

Perform an act of courage that confronts a small fear.

Instructions

- Identify a fear you face in daily life that you usually avoid, such as speaking up in meetings or trying a new activity.

_____

_____

- Challenge yourself to confront this fear within the next week. Plan how and when you'll do it.

_____

_____

_____

- After completing the challenge, reflect on the experience and how it made you feel to step outside your comfort zone.

_____

_____

_____

_____

_____

Activity 2: New Experience Explorer

Objective

Try something completely new to you.

Instructions

- Choose an activity you've never done before but have thought about trying—anything from a cooking class to starting a simple exercise routine.

- Commit to trying this new activity at least once in the next two weeks.

- Write about the experience: *What did you do? How did it feel before, during, and after?*

Activity 3: Facing Fears with Courage

Objective

Create a plan for facing fears with actionable steps.

Instructions

- List your fears in the first column and corresponding actions you can take to face them in the second column.

- Choose one action to focus on in the coming month.

FEAR	ACTIONABLE STEP
ACTION FOR THIS MONTH:	

Journal Prompts

- Write about a moment when you felt intense fear but decided to face it anyway. What was the situation, and what motivated you to take that step?

- Reflect on a time when you allowed fear to stop you from pursuing a goal or trying something new. How might your life be different if you had faced your fear?

- Think of someone you admire for their bravery. What characteristics do they exhibit, and how can you incorporate those traits into your own life?

- Reflect on a past experience where overcoming fear significantly impacted your personal or professional life. How did it change you?

- Write about a fear you faced as a child. How did you confront it, and what did you learn from that experience?

- Think about how fear shapes your daily decisions. What would you do differently if fear wasn't a factor?

"Each time you face that fear, you're growing. You're proving to yourself that you can do it. You're building your confidence muscle."

DEBBIE WEISS

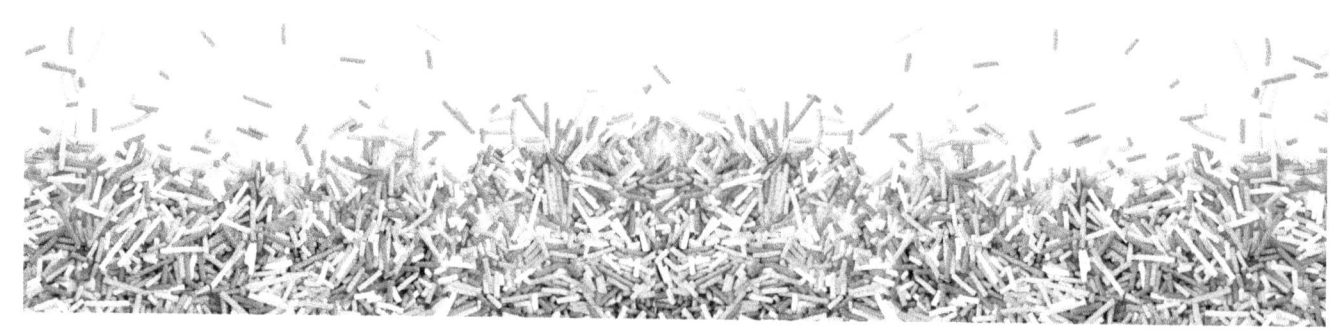

5

A Sprinkle of Responsibility

> **Green:** The color of growth and vitality, green suits the nurturing and sustaining nature of responsibility.

Taking responsibility for your actions is crucial for achieving desired outcomes in life. By focusing on how you respond to events and understanding the E + R = O formula, you can empower yourself to shape your destiny.

Event + Response = Outcome

Owning your choices helps you move away from a victim mentality, promotes accountability, and provides the clarity needed to make more deliberate and beneficial decisions.

Key Takeaways from *The Sprinkle Effect*

1. **Control Your Response:** The E + R = O formula shows us that our power lies in how we respond, not in what happens to us. By focusing on our reactions, we can truly influence the results.

2. **Stepping Up to the Plate:** Realizing that you have a hand in the outcomes of your life through how you respond to events is crucial. It's about owning up to the fact that you're not a passive observer but an active participant in your own story.

3. **Owning Your Choices:** Taking responsibility means recognizing that you hold the steering wheel in your life's journey. This realization is empowering, giving you the freedom to navigate life's ups and downs with confidence and purpose.

Activities

Activity 1: The E+R=O Experiment

Objective

Apply the E+R=O formula to a recent event and analyze the outcome.

Instructions

- Think of a recent situation where you were unhappy with the outcome.

_____

_____

_____

_____

- Write down the event (E), your response (R), and the outcome (O) as it happened.

_____

_____

_____

_____

- Now, brainstorm alternative responses (R) you could have chosen. Write down how each alternative would have potentially changed the outcome (O).

_____

_____

_____

_____

_____

_____

_____

- Reflect on this exercise's insights and how you might apply this awareness to future events.

_____

_____

_____

_____

_____

_____

_____

Activity 2: Choice Mapping

Objective

Visualize how different choices lead to different paths.

Instructions

1. On the following page, write down a choice you're facing in the center circle.

2. Each branch represents a possible decision you can make. Write your various decisions within each branch.

3. Then, continue to branch out further, writing down all possible outcomes of each decision.

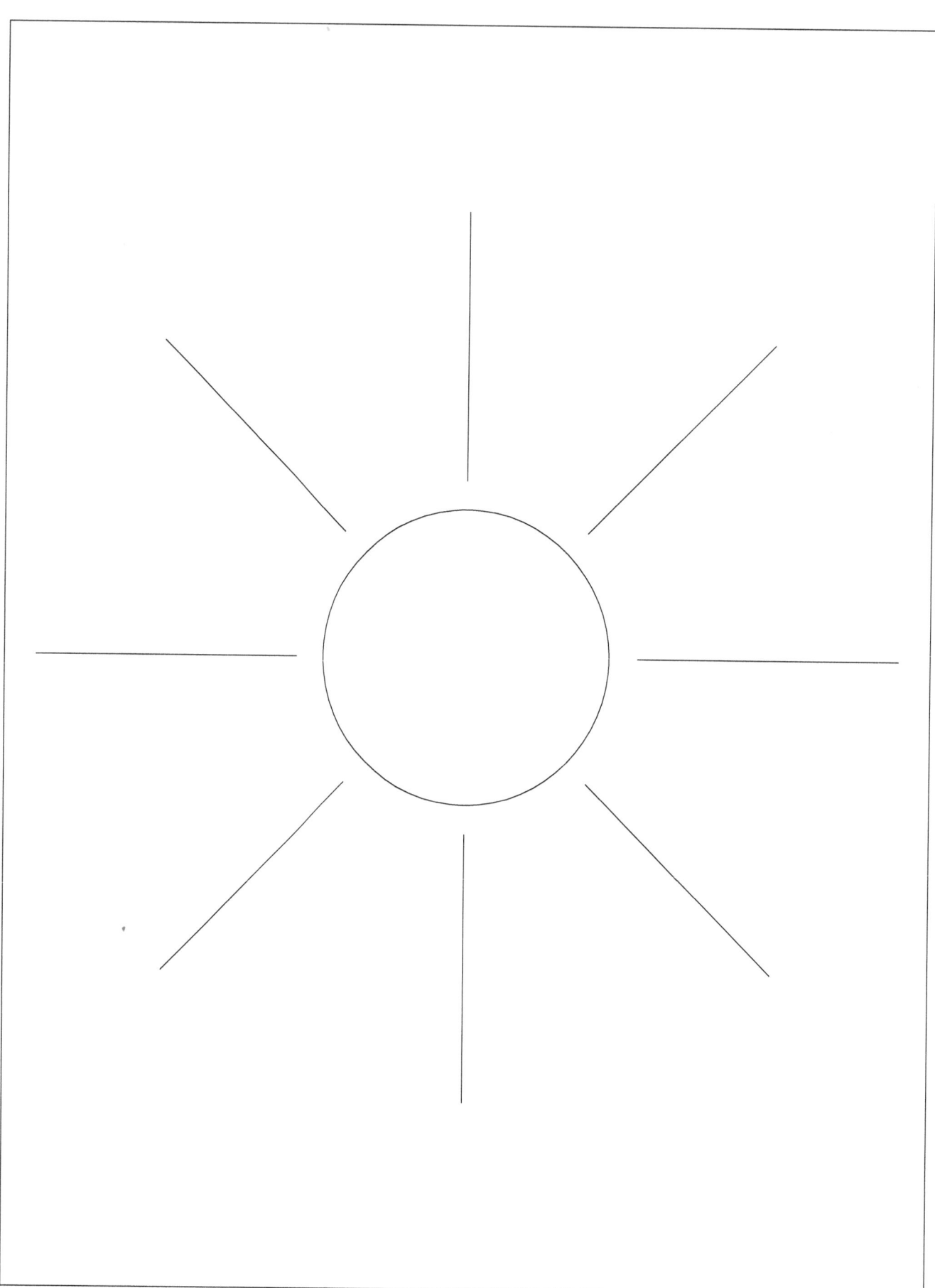

4. Reflect on this map to see how varied your life's path can be based on the choices you make.

_____

_____

_____

_____

_____

_____

_____

_____

Activity 3: Small Changes, Big Impact

Objective

Compile a list of small changes you can make that could lead to significant improvements in your life.

Instructions

- List five small changes you can implement today or this week.

- Next to each, note the impact or outcome you hope to see from making this change.

- At the end of the week or month, review this list and note any progress or insights gained.

CHANGES	OUTCOME
1	
2	
3	
4	
5	

Journal Prompts

- Reflect on a recent event where the outcome was not as you desired. How might a different response from you have changed the outcome?

- Write about a time when you blamed external circumstances for an undesirable outcome. What role did your response play in this situation?

- Identify a current challenge in your life. How can applying the E + R = O formula help you achieve a more favorable outcome?

- Consider a decision you regret. What were the events and responses involved, and how can you use this reflection to make better choices in the future?

- Describe a situation where you took full responsibility for the outcome. How did it feel, and what did you learn from the experience?

- Think about your beliefs around money. How have these beliefs influenced your financial decisions and outcomes?

"I had the power to change my life, one response at a time, and I never knew it."

DEBBIE WEISS

6

A Sprinkle of Dreams

Purple: Often associated with imagination, inspiration, and spirituality, purple evokes a sense of mystery and wonder.

Dreaming big is essential for setting and achieving personal goals. Visualization and belief are key components in turning dreams into reality. By vividly imagining your ideal life and setting clear, actionable goals, you create a roadmap to achieve your aspirations. Dreaming encourages you to think beyond current limitations, fuels your motivation, and inspires you to pursue your passions relentlessly.

Key Takeaways from *The Sprinkle Effect*

1. **Let Yourself Dream:** Don't hold back—imagine the biggest, boldest life you can. Believing in your dreams is the first step to making them come true.

2. **Your Attitude Matters:** How you react to what life throws at you shapes where you end up. Stay positive and see challenges as opportunities to grow.

3. **Act on Your Dreams:** Hope isn't just wishful thinking; it's a call to action. Start small, keep at it, and those big dreams will start to feel a lot closer.

Activities

Activity 1: Dream Visualization

Objective

Vividly visualize and connect with your dream life.

Instructions

- Find a quiet space where you won't be disturbed.

- Close your eyes and imagine your dream life in as much detail as possible. Focus on how this life feels, the sounds around you, the people you're with, and what a typical day looks like. If you have *The Sprinkle Effect*, you can use the prompts in this chapter as a guide.

- Afterwards write about the experience, highlighting the emotions and sensations you felt.

Activity 2: I Can Achieve My Dreams Because...

Objective

Build confidence in your ability to achieve your dreams.

Instructions

- List reasons why you are capable of achieving your dreams, focusing on your strengths, past successes, and resources.

- Add to this list whenever you accomplish something that reinforces your belief in yourself.

Activity 3: Dreams vs. Limiting Beliefs

Objective

Identify and counteract the limiting beliefs holding you back from your dreams.

Instructions

- In the first column, write down your dreams. In the second column, list out the limiting beliefs associated with each dream.

DREAMS	LIMITING BELIEFS

- For each limiting belief, write a counter-statement that challenges and reframes the belief into something positive and empowering.

Journal Prompts

- Reflect on a dream that you've previously set aside as unrealistic or unattainable. What is one small step you could take today that might bring you closer to making this dream a reality? Write about how achieving this dream could transform your life.

- Describe your dream life in detail. Where do you live, what do you do each day, and who are you with? How does this life make you feel?

- Reflect on a dream or goal you had as a child. How has your perspective on this dream changed over the years, and do you still want to pursue it?

- Write about a time when you achieved a dream or goal. What did you learn from this experience, and how can you apply those lessons to your current dreams?

- Imagine what your life would look like if you fully believed in your dreams and your ability to achieve them. How does this belief change your daily actions and decisions?

- Describe an ideal day in your dream life. What activities do you engage in, and how do they contribute to your overall happiness and fulfillment?

"If you don't believe it's possible, then it's not."

DEBBIE WEISS

7

A Sprinkle of Direction

Orange: Vibrant and energetic, orange signifies movement and direction with purpose.

Having clear direction and effective goal-setting strategies are necessary for achieving your ambitions. The S.M.A.R.T. framework (Specific, Measurable, Achievable, Relevant, Time-bound) helps you set realistic and actionable goals. Breaking down larger objectives into smaller, manageable steps ensures steady progress and helps maintain motivation. This structured approach transforms dreams into tangible achievements.

Key Takeaways from *The Sprinkle Effect*

1. **Set S.M.A.R.T. Goals:** Ensure your goals are specific, measurable, achievable, relevant, and time-bound to increase the likelihood of success.

2. **Break It Down:** Divide your ultimate goals into smaller, manageable steps to prevent feeling overwhelmed and to make progress more achievable.

3. **Stay Consistent:** Consistency is key to achieving goals. Start with small steps and maintain a steady effort to gradually build toward your larger aspirations.

Activities

Activity 1: Life Assessment Exercise

Objective

Identify and evaluate current satisfaction levels across various life domains, helping to pinpoint areas needing improvement and setting the stage for targeted goal setting.

Instructions

- List out categories that represent important areas of your life (add to and/or change what's listed).

- Rate your current satisfaction level in each area on a scale of 1 to 10.

- Then, rate where you'd like them to be in your ideal life.

This will help you see where you want to focus your goal-setting efforts.

CATEGORY	RATE YOUR CURRENT SATISFACTION LEVEL ON A SCALE OF 1 TO 10	RATE WHERE YOU'D LIKE THEM TO BE IN YOUR IDEAL LIFE
Career		
Finances		
Spirituality		
Health		
Physical Environment		
Significant Other		
Friends And Family		
Fun		
Personal Growth		

Activity 2: Set S.M.A.R.T. Goals

Objective

Develop clear, structured, and realistic goals for each identified area of improvement, ensuring they are S.M.A.R.T.

For each category you want to improve, set specific, measurable, achievable, relevant, and time-bound goals. This method ensures your goals are clear and reachable within a specific timeframe.

CATEGORY	MY S.M.A.R.T. GOAL IS...
Career	
Finances	
Spirituality	
Health	
Physical Environment	
Significant Other	
Friends And Family	
Fun	
Personal Growth	

Activity 3: Create an Action Plan

Objective

Outline detailed, step-by-step actions required to achieve each S.M.A.R.T. goal, with specific timelines that foster accountability and track progress.

Break down your S.M.A.R.T. goals into smaller, actionable steps. Assign deadlines in one month, six months, and one year, up to your goal-achievement deadline to each step to keep yourself accountable.

CATEGORY	ONE MONTH GOAL	6 MONTH GOAL	ONE YEAR GOAL
Career			
Finances			
Spirituality			
Health			
Physical Environment			
Significant Other			
Friends And Family			
Fun			
Personal Growth			

Journal Prompts

- Think about the potential obstacles you might face in achieving your goals. For each obstacle, write down a strategy or solution to overcome it. This proactive thinking can prepare you for the challenges ahead.

- Pick one area where there's a significant difference between your current satisfaction level and your ideal level. What is one small step you can take today to start bridging that gap?

- Think about a time when you set a goal but didn't achieve it. What were the obstacles, and how can you address these challenges with a new, more effective approach?

- Identify someone in your life or a public figure who excels in an area you want to improve. What steps did they take to get where they are, and how can you incorporate some of their strategies into your own plan?

- Reflect on the power of consistency in achieving your goals. What daily or weekly habits can you develop to move closer to your desired outcomes?

- Write about how having a clear direction through goal setting can transform your life. How does it change your outlook and motivation?

"Your dreams aren't just fantasies; they're a roadmap for your future."

DEBBIE WEISS

8

A Sprinkle of Vision

> **Violet:** Often associated with imagination and spiritual insight, violet is perfect for vision.

Visualization is a powerful tool that can bring your goals within reach. By vividly imagining your success, you create mental pathways that make actual achievement more attainable. Visualization helps you stay focused, motivated, and aligned with your goals, reinforcing the belief that you can achieve what you envision. This technique enhances performance, reduces anxiety, and boosts confidence.

Key Takeaways from *The Sprinkle Effect*

1. **Picture Success:** Visualization helps you see yourself achieving your goals, just like athletes do before a big game.

2. **Use Your Senses:** Make your mental movies vivid by imagining what you see, hear, and feel. The more detailed, the better!

3. **Practice Regularly:** Like any skill, the more you practice visualization, the better you get. Make it a habit to visualize your goals often for maximum impact.

Activities

Activity 1: Guided Visualization

Objective

Use guided imagery to enhance your ability to visualize with the help of a structured audio recording.

Materials Needed

- Access to a guided visualization recording
  (many are available for free online or through apps)

- Headphones

Step 1: Find a Quiet Place

- Ensure you are in a comfortable, quiet space where you won't be disturbed.

Step 2: Select a Guided Visualization

- Choose a recording that best suits your goals. There are general visualizations or those targeted at specific outcomes (like achieving career goals, health, or personal happiness).

Step 3: Listen and Visualize

- Put on your headphones, start the recording, and close your eyes. Follow the narrator's instructions, allowing your imagination to picture what's being described vividly.

Step 4: Visualization Practice

- Regularly practicing guided visualization will train your brain to generate vivid mental images and emotions associated with your desired outcomes, enhancing your focus and motivation.

Activity 2: The "Perfect Day" Scenario

Objective

Develop your visualization skills by imagining your ideal perfect day from start to finish.

Step 1: Find a Comfortable Spot

- Sit in a quiet and comfortable place where you can think without interruptions.

Step 2: Imagine Your Perfect Day

- Close your eyes and imagine your perfect day related to a specific goal you have. Picture everything from the moment you wake up: *What do you see? What are you doing? Who are you with? How do you feel?*

Step 3: Write It Down

- Open your eyes and write down everything you visualized. Describe your surroundings, activities, people, conversations, and especially how you feel throughout the day.

Step 4: Practice Visualization

- Revisit this exercise with varying focuses on different aspects of your life. Regular practice will improve your ability to visualize detailed scenarios, making your mental practice more effective in influencing your subconscious mind.

Activity 3: Vision Board Plus

Objective

Visually represent your dreams and add actionable steps.

Materials Needed

- Magazines,
- Poster board,
- Glue,
- Scissors,
- Markers, and
- Sticky notes.

Instructions

- Create a traditional vision board by cutting out images and words from magazines that align with your dreams and gluing them to the poster board.

- Use sticky notes to write down one action you can take for each image or word to bring you closer to that vision. Stick these notes around the border of your vision board.

- Place your vision board somewhere you will see it every day and make a weekly plan to tackle one of the actions noted on your sticky notes.

Journal Prompts

- Write a letter to yourself five years in the future, imagining that you've achieved all your current dreams. Describe your life, how you feel, and the journey you took to get there. Seal the letter in an envelope and set a date in the future to open it. You might also choose to share this letter with a trusted friend or family member who can send it back to you at the right time.

- Reflect on a recent daydream you had about your future. What details stood out to you, and how did it make you feel?

- Consider an area of your life where you are currently struggling. How could visualizing success in this area help you move forward?

- Describe a time when you used visualization to help you prepare for an event or achieve a goal. What was the outcome, and what did you learn from the experience?

- Identify three sensory details (sight, sound, smell, touch) that you would include in a visualization of achieving one of your biggest goals. How do these details enhance your mental image?

- Write about a personal experience where you felt unprepared for a challenge. How might visualization have helped you feel more prepared and confident?

"Visualization isn't daydreaming; it's a real tool that can help bring your biggest dreams to life."

DEBBIE WEISS

9

A Sprinkle of Action

Magenta: Intense and impactful, magenta represents decisive and dynamic action.

Taking consistent action is essential for turning dreams into reality. By starting with small, manageable steps and staying persistent, you can overcome fear and procrastination. Consistent action, no matter how minor, accumulates over time and leads to significant progress. This approach emphasizes the importance of perseverance and the power of incremental progress in achieving long-term goals.

Key Takeaways from *The Sprinkle Effect*

1. **Start Small:** Tackle your goals with small, manageable steps. This makes the process less daunting and helps you get going without feeling overwhelmed.

2. **Face Your Fears:** Don't let the fear of messing up hold you back. Remember, taking action is always better than doing nothing. Every step forward is progress.

3. **Stay Consistent:** Keep at it, even if the steps are tiny. Regular effort adds up, turning small actions into big achievements over time. It's all about keeping the momentum going!

Activities

Activity 1: The Micro-Action Plan

Objective

Initiate progress towards a goal through micro-actions.

Instructions

- Choose a goal or project you've been putting off.

Goal:

_____

_____

_____

_____

- Break down the goal into the smallest possible actions, actions so small that they seem almost too easy to accomplish.

_____

_____

_____

_____

- Commit to completing one micro-action per day. Track your progress using the grid below and celebrate each step, no matter how small.

Days	1	2	3	4	5	6	7	8	9	10	11	12	13	14	15	16	17	18	19	20	21	22	23	24	25	26	27	28	29	30
Goal																														

Activity 2: Daily Intentions Journal

Objective

Set daily intentions that support your larger goals and reflect on your progress to continuously improve your effectiveness and productivity.

Start each day by writing down one to three small intentions that align with your larger goals. These should be specific, achievable actions you can complete within the day.

Review these intentions at the end of the day to reflect on your progress. If you were unable to accomplish them, analyze why so you can adjust the following day. Either use the space below, a physical notebook, or a digital document, whatever feels most comfortable and accessible.

Activity 3: The 5-Minute Challenge

Objective

Overcome procrastination and kickstart action by tackling tasks that can be completed in just five minutes.

Instructions

1. Make a list of small tasks related to your goals that can be completed in five minutes or less.

2. Each day, randomly select one task from your list and commit to completing it within five minutes.

3. Use a timer to keep yourself on track. The pressure of the timer can help you focus your efforts and make the task feel like a fun challenge.

4. After completing the task, note how it felt to accomplish something quickly and how it contributed to your larger goals.

5. Gradually increase the complexity or duration of tasks as you build confidence and momentum for taking action.

5-MINUTE TASK	HOW IT FELT TO COMPLETE IT

Journal Prompts

- Reflect on a time when you felt overwhelmed by a large task. How did breaking it down into smaller steps help, or how could it have helped?

- Write about a fear that's holding you back from taking action. What can you do to face this fear and push through it?

- Think about a project you started but never finished. What were the obstacles, and how can you overcome similar challenges in the future?

- Describe a time when you successfully pushed through fear and took action. What was the outcome, and how did it change your perspective on taking action?

- Reflect on the difference between planning and action. How can you balance planning with taking decisive steps toward your goals?

- List three ways taking consistent small actions has improved your life. How can you apply this strategy to other areas where you want to see progress?

"Without action, everything that came before are just dreams and plans."

DEBBIE WEISS

10

A Sprinkle of Discipline

> **Gray:** Steady and unwavering, gray reflects the stability and structure of discipline.

Discipline is key to long-term success and personal growth. Establishing routines, maintaining accountability, and persevering through challenges help build and sustain discipline. Consistent effort and self-control ensure you will stay on track to achieve your goals. Discipline fosters resilience, enhances productivity, and helps you develop the habits necessary for sustained success.

Key Takeaways from *The Sprinkle Effect*

1. **Find Your Why:** Understanding your deeper motivation helps sustain discipline. Knowing why you're pursuing a goal provides clarity and fuels your perseverance, especially when challenges arise.

2. **Set Up Routines:** A consistent routine can be a game-changer. It puts you in control and sets the tone for a productive day, helping you stick to your plan and move closer to your goals.

3. **Seek Support:** Don't do it alone! Finding someone to share your journey with can make a huge difference. An accountability partner not only motivates you but also celebrates your successes and supports you through challenges.

Activities

Activity 1: The Accountability Pact

Objective

Build accountability for taking consistent action towards your goals.

Instructions

- Identify a friend, family member, or coworker who also has a goal they're working towards.

- Make a pact to hold each other accountable for taking daily or weekly steps towards your respective goals.

- Schedule a regular check-in to update each other on your progress, challenges, and successes.

Activity 2: The Distraction List

Objective

Identify and mitigate distractions that hinder your ability to maintain discipline.

Instructions

1. Over the course of one week, keep a log of moments when you find yourself distracted from your tasks.

2. Categorize these distractions (e.g., social media, unnecessary interruptions, multitasking).

3. At the end of the week, review your list and determine which distractions are the most frequent.

4. Develop a strategy to reduce or eliminate these top distractions from your work environment.

Activity 3: The 21-Day Discipline Challenge

Objective

Establish and reinforce a new habit that contributes to your larger goal.

Instructions

- Choose one small action you can take every day that will build discipline and contribute to your goal (e.g., waking up at a certain time, exercising for 30 minutes, reading industry-related material for 15 minutes).

_____

_____

_____

- Commit to doing this action every day for 21 days, tracking your progress below.

- Reflect daily on how this activity is helping to build your discipline and how it's impacting your progress towards your goals.

DAY	REFLECTION	✓
1		
2		
3		
4		
5		
6		
7		

8		
9		
10		
11		
12		
13		
14		
15		
16		
17		
18		
19		
20		
21		

Journal Prompts

- Reflect on a past experience where maintaining discipline led to a positive outcome. What strategies did you use to stay focused, and how can you apply them to current challenges?

- Write down your "Why" for pursuing your current goals. What is the deeper motivation behind your efforts?

- Think about a recent setback. How can adopting a disciplined approach help you overcome similar challenges in the future?

- Identify a person in your life or someone you admire who exemplifies discipline. What can you learn from their habits and apply to your own life?

- Write about a time when you lacked discipline and the impact it had on your progress. How can you use this experience to build stronger habits moving forward?

- Reflect on a daily affirmation that inspires you to stay disciplined. How can you incorporate this affirmation into your routine to maintain motivation?

"Commitment is doing the thing you said you would do, long after the mood you said it in has left you."

GEORGE ZALUCKI

A Sprinkle of Adaptability

> **Teal:** Fluid and versatile, teal mirrors the flexibility and adaptiveness required in change.

Adaptability is crucial for thriving in a world of constant change. Being flexible and open to new paths allows you to turn setbacks into growth opportunities. By continuously evaluating and adjusting your strategies, you can navigate through life's uncertainties and seize new opportunities. Adaptability promotes resilience, encourages innovation, and helps you maintain a positive outlook despite challenges.

Key Takeaways from *The Sprinkle Effect*

1. **Embrace Flexibility:** Life's unexpected challenges are opportunities to learn and grow. Being flexible allows you to navigate these challenges effectively, continually progressing towards your goals.

2. **Reframe Setbacks as Lessons:** Like Thomas Edison's approach to inventing the light bulb, view each setback as a step closer to success, not as a failure. This mindset transforms obstacles into steppingstones.

3. **Adaptability Is Essential for Growth:** Constantly evaluate and adjust your strategies in response to life's changes. This adaptability not only helps in overcoming obstacles but also in seizing new opportunities that arise.

Activities

Activity 1: Embrace the Obstacle

Objective

Transform obstacles into opportunities for growth.

Steps

- Identify a significant obstacle you're currently facing.

- Consider how this obstacle can be viewed as an opportunity for learning or direction change. Ask yourself what new skills, insights, or connections you can gain from addressing this challenge.

- Write a plan that includes at least one actionable step you can take to leverage this obstacle as a growth opportunity.

Activity 2: The Adaptability Journal

Objective

Cultivate a mindset that embraces change and adaptability.

Instructions

- Keep a daily or weekly journal to write about and reflect on moments where you had to adapt to unexpected circumstances. Either use the space below, a physical notebook, or a digital document, whatever feels most comfortable and accessible.

- For each entry, note the situation, how you adapted (or struggled to adapt), and what you learned from the experience.

- Regularly review your journal entries to identify patterns in how you deal with change and areas where you can improve your adaptability.

Activity 3: Feedback Loops

Objective

Actively seek and integrate feedback for continuous adaptation.

Steps

- Choose an area of your life or a specific project where feedback could be beneficial.

- Identify at least three people whose opinions you value and ask them for specific feedback on this area or project.

- Analyze the feedback for common themes and identify one action you can take to adjust based on this feedback.

Journal Prompts

- Write about a time when being flexible or changing your plan led to an unexpected success. How did adaptability play a role in this outcome?

- Reflect on a recent situation where you had to adapt quickly. What was the challenge, and how did you navigate it?

- Think of a time when a setback turned out to be a valuable learning experience. What did you learn, and how did it help you grow?

- Identify an area in your life where you struggle with change. What steps can you take to become more adaptable in this area?

- List the benefits of being adaptable. How can embracing flexibility positively impact your personal and professional life?

- Describe a situation where being too rigid resulted in a missed opportunity. How could adaptability have changed the outcome?

"Don't get discouraged
by setbacks; instead, use
them as opportunities
to grow and learn."

DEBBIE WEISS

12

A Sprinkle of Resilience

> **Indigo:** Deep and resilient, indigo reflects the inner strength and endurance of resilience.

Resilience is the ability to bounce back from adversity and grow stronger amidst challenges. Building mental and emotional strength through practices like gratitude, self-care, and mindfulness helps you navigate life's ups and downs effectively. Resilience enables you to face challenges with confidence, recover from setbacks quickly, and maintain a positive perspective, ultimately leading to a more fulfilling life.

Key Takeaways from *The Sprinkle Effect*

1. **Understanding Resilience:** Resilience is our ability to bounce back from tough times. It helps us grow stronger and keep a positive outlook, no matter what we face.

2. **Learning from Others:** Just like Nelson Mandela's perseverance transformed his life and impacted the world, our struggles teach us valuable lessons about strength and courage.

3. **It's a Journey:** Building resilience doesn't happen overnight. It involves taking care of ourselves, reaching out for support, and finding tools like journaling to help us reflect and heal.

Activities

Activity 1: Free-form Journaling

Objective

Get out your thoughts and feelings in a safe way.

Instructions

- Write for a minimum of five minutes with no agenda. If you don't know what to write, keep writing "I don't know what to write" until you eventually move on to something else.

- Try this three to five times before deciding whether or not you find this tool useful. Many find it takes practice. Don't give up on the first go.

Activity 2: The Support Circle

Objective

Recognize and lean on your support network.

Instructions

- Make a list of people (family, friends, or community members) who have supported you in the past or whom you believe could support you now.

- Next to each name, write down how they can help you (listening, advice, or practical help) and how you might reach out to them.

- Commit to contacting at least one person from this list within the next week to seek support or simply connect.

Activity 3: Learning from Loss

Objective

Process feelings of loss and identify growth.

Instructions

- Reflect on a loss you have experienced and write about it, focusing not just on the pain but also on any growth or learning that came from it.

- Identify specific strengths you discovered in yourself as a result of dealing with this loss.

- Consider how you can apply these strengths in other areas of your life moving forward.

Journal Prompts

- Reflect on your day-to-day activities. Identify a moment today where you demonstrated resilience, no matter how small the instance. How did it feel to persevere, and what did you learn about yourself?

- Reflect on a recent challenge you faced. How did you navigate through it, and what did you learn about yourself?

- Identify a time when you felt like giving up but didn't. What kept you going, and what was the outcome?

- Write about a significant loss or setback you've experienced. How did this experience shape you, and what strengths did you discover as a result?

- List three personal strengths that have helped you during tough times. How can you leverage these strengths in future challenges?

- Consider the role of self-care in resilience. What self-care practices can you incorporate into your daily routine to enhance your resilience?

"Resilience is more than just bouncing back from adversity. It's our ability to move through difficult times, learn from them, and continue to grow and thrive."

BRENÉ BROWN

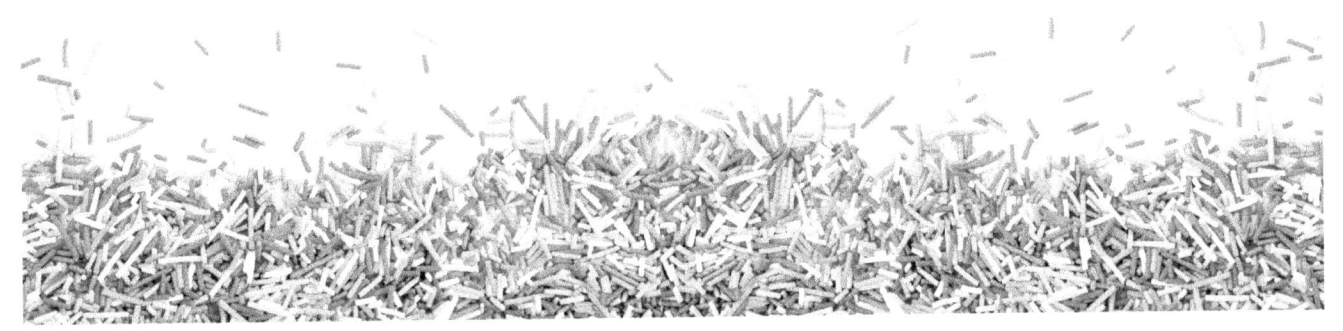

13

A Sprinkle of Curiosity

Lime Green: Fresh and zesty, lime green captures the essence of curiosity and the thirst for knowledge.

Curiosity is a powerful driver of personal growth and discovery. Maintaining a curious mindset encourages you to explore new ideas, experiences, and perspectives. Embracing curiosity leads to continuous learning, fosters creativity, and opens up a world of possibilities. By following your curiosity, you can break free from routine, challenge your assumptions, and create a richer, more fulfilling life.

Key Takeaways from *The Sprinkle Effect*

1. **Try New Things:** Jumping into new activities, even if they feel a bit out of reach, can really boost both your physical and mental well-being. For example, starting yoga might be tough at first, but the benefits for your back and peace of mind can be undeniable.

2. **Let Curiosity Lead:** Allowing your curiosity to guide you can open up a world of new experiences, enriching your life significantly. Whether it's a new hobby or cultural exploration, it makes every day more exciting and fulfilling.

3. **Face Your Fears:** By actively engaging in new experiences, you'll start to dismantle your fears and build real confidence. From experimenting with different healing techniques to exploring philosophical ideas, taking these steps can transform your outlook and strengthen your spirit.

Activities

Activity 1: Curiosity Quest

Objective

Embark on a journey of discovery, exploring new hobbies, practices, or knowledge areas.

Instructions

1. List five activities or subjects you've always been curious about but haven't explored. These could range from artistic endeavors like painting or writing, to physical activities such as yoga or hiking, to academic interests like learning a new language or exploring astronomy.

2. Choose one from your list and commit to trying it out within the next month.

3. Research local classes, online tutorials, or simply start with books from the library.

4. Journal about your experience, noting how it felt to try something new, what you learned, and whether it's something you'd like to continue.

Activity 2: Daily Wonder Walk

Objective

Cultivate mindfulness and an observant eye towards the everyday world.

Instructions

- Take a daily walk, but with the specific intention of noticing five new things you haven't seen before. These could be as simple as the color of a neighbor's door, a plant growing through a crack in the sidewalk, or the way the light casts shadows at a certain time of day.

- After your walk, spend a few minutes writing about these observations and how they might relate to the broader world or your inner life.

Activity 3: Idea Exploration Journal

Objective

Create a dedicated space for exploring new ideas and reflections.

Instructions

- Start an "Idea Exploration Journal." Either use the space below, a physical notebook, or a digital document, whatever feels most comfortable and accessible.

- Whenever you encounter a new idea that sparks interest—whether from a book, conversation, podcast, etc.—make a note of it in your journal. Write down why it intrigues you and how you might explore it further.

- Commit to revisiting one of these ideas each week, dedicating time to learning more about it through further research, experimentation, or reflection.

Journal Prompts

- Reflect on what fascinated you as a child. Are there elements of those early curiosities that you still find intriguing today? How can you reconnect with those interests now?

- Reflect on a time when you tried something new. What was the experience like, and what did you learn from it?

- Think of a belief or assumption you've held about yourself or the world. What evidence can you find that challenges this belief?

- Describe a recent "aha" moment when a newfound piece of knowledge or experience shifted your perspective. What led to this moment, and how did it change your thinking?

- What are three questions you have about the world around you right now? How can you begin to seek answers to these questions?

- Consider an area of your life where you feel stuck. How might approaching it with curiosity open up new possibilities?

"Shifting my mindset from
"I can't" to *"maybe I can"*
was life-changing."

DEBBIE WEISS

14

A Sprinkle of Connection

Pink: Warm and inviting, pink is ideal for the nurturing aspect of connection.

Building meaningful connections with others is vital for personal and emotional well-being. Supportive communities and relationships provide encouragement, accountability, and a sense of belonging. Nurturing positive connections promotes growth, happiness, and resilience. By surrounding yourself with like-minded individuals, you can enhance your support network and enrich your life.

Key Takeaways from *The Sprinkle Effect*

1. **Strength In Community:** Being part of groups like Weight Watchers or a support group for parents of children with autism shows how shared challenges can bring people together, offering support and inspiration.

2. **Choose Your Circle Wisely:** The people you hang out with can really shape your life. Spending time with positive folks can boost your mood and help you reach your goals.

3. **Setting Boundaries:** It's okay to have limits with friends and family who don't see eye-to-eye with you. Clear boundaries help keep these relationships healthy without stopping your personal progress.

Activities

Activity 1: Connecting with New People

Objective

Identify people you've wanted to meet but have been hesitant to approach, and create a simple plan to connect with them.

Step 1: Find a Comfortable Spot

- Sit in a quiet and comfortable place where you can think without interruptions.

Step 2: Imagine Your Perfect Day

- Close your eyes and imagine your perfect day related to a specific goal you have. Picture everythi

Step 1: Reflect on Your Current Circle

- List Five People: Who do you spend the most time with? Next to each name, note if they uplift or drain you.

_____

_____

_____

Step 2: Identify Potential Connections

- List New People: Write down the names of people you want to meet and why you're interested in them.

_____

_____

_____

Step 3: Face Your Fears

- Note the Hesitation: Write down what has stopped you from reaching out to each person in the past.

- Challenge the Fear: Counter each fear with a positive thought.

_____

_____

Step 4: Make a Plan

- Decide how you'll reach out - phone, email, or in person.

- Draft Your Message: Keep it simple and genuine.

- Set a Deadline: Pick a date to reach out by.

Step 5: Reflect on the Outcome

- Note the Experience: How did it go? What did you learn?

- Adjust if Needed: If it didn't go as planned, think about how to improve next time.

Activity 2: Community Exploration Exercise

Objective

Physically connect with communities that share your interests or values, enriching your social life and expanding your network.

Instructions

1. Research local clubs, organizations, or groups that align with your interests. You can use online resources, community boards, or local event listings.

2. Make a list of these groups, jotting down contact information and meeting times.

3. Choose one group from your list and commit to attending a meeting or event within the next month.

4. Prepare a few questions or topics of discussion for when you attend to ensure you engage actively.

5. Reflect on your experience afterwards to determine if this group feels like a good fit for your personal and social growth.

Activity 3: Join Online Forums

Objective

Digitally engage with communities that share your interests, providing you with a platform to learn, share, and grow.

Instructions

- Identify online forums, social media groups, or platforms that focus on your areas of interest.

- Create an account on one or more of these platforms if you haven't already.

- Start by reading existing discussions to get a feel for the community's tone and topics.

- Actively participate by posting your own insights, responding to others' posts, or asking questions. Aim to make at least one post and two comments in your first week.

- Evaluate after a week if your chosen platforms add value to your knowledge and whether the community engagement is beneficial to your growth.

Journal Prompts

- Reflect on a time when being part of a group or community had a positive impact on your life. What did you gain from that experience?

- Think about a relationship in your life that drains your energy. What boundaries can you set to protect your well-being?

- Write about a recent interaction that made you feel deeply connected to someone. What elements contributed to that sense of connection?

- Consider the quote by Jim Rohn: "You are the average of the five people you spend the most time with." Who are your five, and how do they influence your life?

- Write about a time when you supported someone through a difficult period. How did this strengthen your relationship with them?

- Think about the qualities that you value in your closest friends. How do these qualities contribute to your personal growth and happiness?

"Regularly taking stock of your relationships to ensure they are still positive and supportive is essential."

DEBBIE WEISS

15

A Sprinkle of Joy

> **Yellow:** Often seen as bright, cheerful, and uplifting, yellow symbolizes happiness, positivity, and warmth.

Cultivating joy is essential for overall well-being. Practices like gratitude and positivity help you find happiness in everyday moments. Integrating these practices into your daily routine shifts your focus from what's lacking to what you do have, boosting your overall sense of fulfillment. By appreciating the little things, you can enhance your outlook on life and increase your overall happiness.

Key Takeaways from *The Sprinkle Effect*

1. **Gratitude Reveals Hidden Joys:** The practice of gratitude can lead to the discovery of joy in unexpected places. By focusing on what you're thankful for, you may start to notice the small, often overlooked details in your daily life that bring happiness, leading to a deeper appreciation for the present moment.

2. **Gratitude Can Change Your Outlook:** Even if you're skeptical at first, regularly writing down what you're thankful for can transform your outlook. It turns out that noticing and appreciating the simple things can make life feel richer and more enjoyable.

3. **Spreading Gratitude Feels Great:** Sharing your gratitude isn't just good for you; it lifts others up, too. Whether it's a smile, a thank you, or a kind note, showing gratitude makes a big difference in your community and circles.

Activities

Activity 1: Gratitude Morning Kick-Off

Objective

Begin each day with a mindset focused on gratitude, positively impacting your mood and outlook.

Instructions

- Each morning, before getting out of bed or while in the bathroom, mentally list three things you're grateful for. These can be as simple as the comfort of your bed, the sunshine peeking through your window, or a specific person in your life.

- Reflect on why each of these things brings you joy or comfort, delving a bit deeper into the feeling of gratitude.

Activity 2: Happiness Habit Tracker

Objective

Identify and cultivate personal habits that contribute to your happiness.

Instructions

- Create a list of activities that make you feel happy and fulfilled. Include both simple, daily activities and more significant, less frequent ones.

- Use a habit tracker (either a physical tracker in a planner or a digital app) to monitor how often you engage in these happiness-boosting activities. Aim to incorporate at least one into your daily routine.

Activity 3: Acts of Kindness Day

Objective

Experience the joy of giving through random acts of kindness.

Instructions

- Designate one day each month as your "Acts of Kindness Day." Plan ahead by listing acts of kindness you can easily carry out, such as leaving a positive note for someone, paying for the person behind you in line at the coffee shop, or donating to a local charity.

- Reflect on how each act of kindness made you feel and the reactions you received. This can further cement the positive impact such actions have on your own sense of well-being.

Journal Prompts

- Reflect on a recent moment that brought you pure joy. What was happening, and how did it make you feel?

- Think about a time when you were skeptical about a practice (like gratitude journaling) but decided to try it anyway. What was the outcome?

- Describe a small, everyday activity that brings you joy. How can you incorporate more of this activity into your routine?

- Identify a simple pleasure that you often overlook. How can you become more mindful of this joy in your daily life?

- Reflect on a time when you spread joy to others. How did it make you feel, and what impact did it have on those around you?

- Think about a place that makes you feel happy and at peace. Describe it in detail and explore why it brings you joy.

"So, from someone who once doubted it, I can say gratitude really does work—it makes life richer and more fulfilling."

DEBBIE WEISS

You did it!

I'm so proud of you, but more importantly, you should be proud of yourself for putting in the time and effort necessary to uncover the more colorful and fulfilling life that has been waiting for you. Do you now see how you held the key all along? I've provided the framework, but you are the only one who determines how you live and enjoy the remainder of your life.

I'm on the same journey you are, and we will both continue that journey until we take our last breath. My own voyage has led me to become a writer and speaker—two titles I never even dreamt would be used to describe me. Have any new doors opened for you? If not, I promise they will reveal themselves as you continue your adventure.

My hope is this is just the beginning for you. I am here to help you in any way I can. Since I, too, am evolving, you never know what new resources I have available to help you down this new path. Please make sure to visit www.debbieRweiss.com often to explore new tools and resources.

If you'd like to know more about my own journey, make sure to check out my memoir, *On Second Thought...Maybe I Can!* I know it will inspire and motivate you to stay the course. I'm going to end with the quote which has become my north star. It's from Glinda the Good Witch in *The Wizard of Oz*:

"You've always had the power my dear, you just had to learn it for yourself."

Keep going,

Debbie

Debbie Weiss

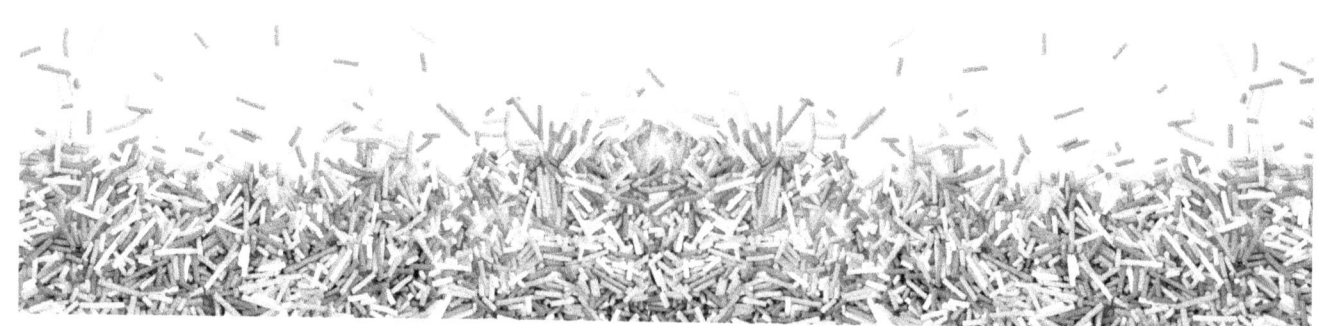

About the Author

Debbie is a bestselling author, speaker, coach, and course creator with over sixty years of experience overcoming life's challenges. As a family caregiver for over forty years, a widow, and the mother of two boys in their twenties, Debbie draws from deep personal experience in her mission to help others. She is the author of the memoir *On Second Thought, Maybe I Can...* and a contributor to the Amazon bestseller *Heart Whispers.* In addition to her writing, Debbie operates an insurance agency and runs the online store **A Sprinkle of Hearts.** She also hosts the **Maybe I Can** podcast, where she shares her journey and insights to inspire others.

Debbie is a Certified Canfield Trainer in **The Success Principles,** bringing a wealth of knowledge and proven strategies to her coaching and presentations. She is passionate about helping people overcome their limiting beliefs and fears, lose the victim mentality, and take control of their lives despite their circumstances. Whether through her books, courses, or speaking engagements, Debbie aims to unlock the potential in every individual she connects with.

In her leisure time, she enjoys traveling, going to the beach, reading, and staying active. Debbie's ultimate mission is to inspire others to embrace their unique journeys and create a more colorful and fulfilled life.